PANCAKES MATTER!

Written by Amy Schumacher Hall — Illustrated by Doris Ettlinger

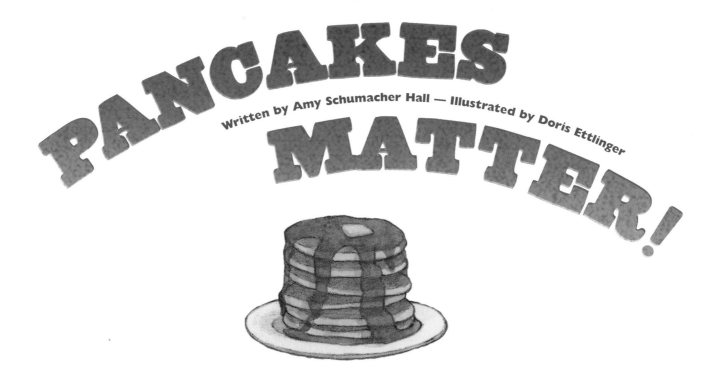

Think of your favorite kind of pancakes. Are they blueberry, chocolate chip, or do you like them plain with maple syrup?

2

Whatever flavor, they are made of **matter**.
Everything on Earth is made of matter.

Making pancakes is a good way to learn about **solids**, **liquids**, and **gases**. These are the three **states** of matter.

To make pancakes we need flour, sugar, and vanilla.
We also need baking powder, milk, and beaten eggs.

The table, the bowl, and the whisk are solids.

Which **ingredients** are solids?

All Purpose FLOUR

PURE GRANULATED SUGAR

Baking Powder

Flour, sugar, and baking powder are solids. Each **grain** stays the same shape unless you do something to it.

Which ingredients are liquids?

Can you guess?

Milk, vanilla, and beaten eggs are liquids because they change shape to fit their container. Are any of the ingredients a gas?

Remember that most gases are invisible. You don't add any gases when making pancakes.

But the bubbles that form as the pancakes cook are full of air. Air is a gas.

Come and get it!